Design: Art of Design
Recipe Photography: Peter Barry
Jacket and Illustration Artwork: Jane Winton, courtesy
of Bernard Thornton Artists, London
Editors: Jillian Stewart and Kate Cranshaw

CLB 3519
Published by Grange Books, an imprint of Grange Books
PLC, The Grange, Grange Yard, London, SE1 3AG
© 1994 CLB Publishing, Godalming, Surrey, England.
Printed and bound in Singapore
Published 1994
ISBN 1-85627-439-X

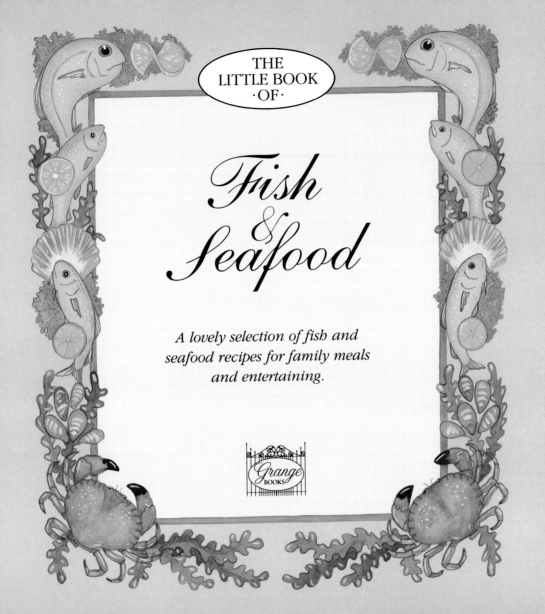

THE
LITTLE BOOK
·OF·

Fish & Seafood

*A lovely selection of fish and
seafood recipes for family meals
and entertaining.*

Grange
BOOKS

Introduction

Fish and seafood is undergoing something of a resurgence in popularity. For some people it is the obvious alternative to meat; others will be attracted by its healthy image; most will enjoy fish simply for the delicious and varied tastes that it offers. Fish is just as high in protein as meat, and is lighter and easier to digest. It is also a good source of important vitamins and minerals. There are many excellent reasons for eating more fish, and in recognition of this, most large supermarkets carry good stocks of fresh fish, both familiar and exotic. Where there is no fresh fish available, there is certainly always canned fish, and this, too, can be used in a many different ways.

Versatility is one of the great attributes of fish. As well as being suitable for cooking in countless different ways, it is also a wonderful main ingredient for any occasion, whether for family lunch in the form of a soup or quiche, grilled for a light evening meal, or served in a wine or cream sauce at a special dinner party.

One of the drawbacks of buying fish and shellfish used to be the laborious and messy cleaning involved in the preparation. Not only is fish now more readily available, but it is also usually cleaned and prepared for cooking by the fishmonger. Shellfish, too, is available in ever greater variety and conveniently prepared for the modern kitchen.

It is important to be able to tell good fresh fish and seafood from that which has been frozen and thawed repeatedly. Fresh fish should always be the first choice for the best taste and texture, but where this is not practical, fish that has been frozen need not be passed over. A really fresh fish is slimy and slithery with a bright eye with black pupil, firm flesh and clean red gills. A stale fish looks dull, has sunken eyes with grey pupils and dirty, dark gills. Shellfish should look clean and bright. Cooked prawns and crabs should be bright red. Lobsters and crabs should be good and heavy, and the tail and claws should still be springy, indicating that they were alive before being boiled. Shellfish such as mussels and oysters should be firmly closed if bought alive. Any open shells indicate that the creature is dead and must therefore be discarded.

A freshly caught fish is wonderful eaten with little or no adornment, such as a trout cooked over a campfire, or sardines eaten on the harbour front with chunks of fresh bread and lemon quarters. However, in ordinary domestic circumstances it is fun to blend fish with new flavours and to experiment with herbs and spices. This inspiring selection of easy and attractive recipes just begs to be tried, and will surely convince you that, as well as being healthy, fish is one of the most underrated and delicious foods available.

Smoked Mackerel Pâté

SERVES 4

Smoked fish has a wonderful flavour and is ideal for making pâté.

PREPARATION: 30 mins, plus 30 mins chilling

225g/8oz smoked mackerel fillets, skin and
    bones removed
60g/2oz margarine
Juice of ½ orange
1 tsp tomato purée
1 tsp white wine vinegar
Salt and freshly ground black pepper, optional
1 × 113g/3½ oz can pimento peppers, drained
280ml/½ pint clear vegetable stock
2 tsps powdered gelatine
2 tbsps dry sherry
2 tbsps cold water

1. Put the mackerel, margarine, orange juice,
tomato purée, vinegar and seasonings into a

Step 2 Arrange the strips of pimento in a lattice pattern over the top of the pâté.

Step 4 Sprinkle the gelatine over the hot stock and allow it to stand, to dissolve completely.

liquidiser or food processor and blend until
smooth.

2. Put the pâté into a serving dish and smooth
the top evenly. Cut the pimentos into thin strips
and arrange in a lattice over the top of the pâté.

3. Bring the stock to the boil in a small pan.
Remove from the heat and cool for 1 minute.

4. Sprinkle over the gelatine and allow to
stand, stirring occasionally until it has
completely dissolved. When the liquid is clear,
stir in the sherry and cold water.

5. Very carefully spoon the aspic over the top
of the mackerel pâté and the pimentos, taking
great care not to dislodge the lattice pattern.
Chill until the aspic has completely set.

Mussels in White Wine

SERVES 3-4

Mussels make a delicious starter to a meal and are quick to prepare.

PREPARATION: 20 mins
COOKING: 6-8 mins

---

60 live mussels
1 large onion, or 4 shallots, finely chopped
½ bottle dry white wine
2 tsps plain flour
2 tsps butter
Salt and pepper
Pinch of ground nutmeg
2 tbsps parsley, chopped

---

1. Wash and scrub the mussels well, discarding any that are open and will not close when lightly tapped. Place the mussels in a large saucepan, add the onion or shallots, and wine.

2. Cover and bring to the boil. Cook for about 5 minutes, shaking the saucepan from time to time, until all the mussels are open.

3. Strain the liquor into another saucepan. Remove the top shells from the mussels and put the mussels into warmed soup plates; keep warm.

4. Work the flour into the butter and add in small pieces to the strained liquor. Bring to the boil, whisking constantly as it thickens. Season to taste with salt, pepper and nutmeg. Add the parsley and pour over the mussels.

Devilled Crabs

SERVES 6

Crab makes an ideal starter for a dinner party.

PREPARATION: 35 mins
COOKING: 15 mins

---

6 boiled crabs
15g/½oz butter
2 tbsps flour
225ml/8 fl oz double cream
2 tsps mustard powder
1 tsp Worcestershire sauce
Salt and pepper
4 hard-boiled eggs
Dry breadcrumbs
Melted butter
Chopped parsley

---

1. Break off all the crab claws. Crack the large claws and legs and pick out the meat. Reserve the smaller legs. Break the crabmeat into pieces and discard any cartilage and shell.

2. Separate the bodies from the large shells. Discard the spongy 'fingers' and the stomach which is found just under the head. Pick out all the meat and combine it with the claw meat. Clean the upper shells thoroughly.

3. Melt the butter and add the flour, stirring well. Stir in the cream, mustard and Worcestershire sauce. Cook over moderate heat, stirring constantly, until thickened. Add salt and pepper to taste.

4. Chop the hard-boiled eggs and add to the sauce with the crabmeat. Spoon into the clean shells, sprinkle lightly with breadcrumbs and drizzle with melted butter.

5. Bake in an oven preheated to 180°C/350°F/Gas Mark 4 for about 10 minutes, or until golden brown. Sprinkle with some chopped parsley and serve surrounded by the reserved crab legs.

Taramasalata

SERVES 4

This well known, classic Greek starter is a delicious way of improving your intake of vitamins B and C.

PREPARATION: 15-25 mins, plus 30 mins chilling

90g/3oz smoked cod roe
6 slices white bread, crusts removed
Juice of 1 lemon
1 small onion, finely chopped
90ml/6 tbsps olive oil
Black olives and chopped fresh parsley, for
　garnish

1. Cut the cod roe in half and scrape out the centre into a bowl. Discard the skin.

2. Put the bread into a bowl along with 140ml/¼ pint warm water. Allow the bread to soak for about 10 minutes, then drain off the water and squeeze the bread until it is almost dry. Add the

Step 2 Soak the bread for about 10 minutes, drain off the water and squeeze the bread until almost dry.

Step 4
Gradually add the oil to the fish mixture, beating continuously and very vigorously between additions to prevent curdling.

bread to the bowl containing the roe and stir in with the lemon juice.

3. Put the cod roe mixture into a blender or food processor, along with the onion. Process until the ingredients form a smooth paste.

4. Return the blended mixture to a bowl and gradually beat in the oil, a little at a time, as if making mayonnaise. Beat the mixture very thoroughly between additions with a whisk or wooden spoon.

5. Refrigerate for at least ½ hour to chill thoroughly, then transfer to a serving bowl and garnish with the black olives and chopped parsley.

Sole Surprise

SERVES 4

Serve these tasty fish parcels with new potatoes and broccoli.

PREPARATION: 25 mins
COOKING: 40 mins

225g/8oz puff pastry
225g/8oz frozen spinach, defrosted
60g/2oz butter
4 small or 2 large fillets of sole, skinned

Sauce
30g/1oz butter
2 tbsps plain flour
340ml/12 fl oz milk
Pinch of diced dill
Salt and pepper
60g/2oz grated cheese

1. Roll the pastry out into a rectangle 12.5 × 20cm/5 × 8 inches. Cut into four equal-size rectangles 6.25 × 10cm/2½ × 4 inches.

2. Fold the rectangles over, short sides together. Cut out the centres with a sharp knife, leaving 1.25cm/½-inch all round. Roll out the centre pieces on a floured board until they are the same size as the 'frames'.

3. Brush the edges with milk and put the 'frames' on the base. Brush the tops with milk and place on a greased baking sheet. Bake in an oven preheated to 220°C/425°F/Gas Mark 7, for 10-15 minutes or until well risen and golden brown.

4. Meanwhile, put the spinach in a pan with 5mm/¼-inch water and a little salt. Cover and cook for 4-5 minutes. Drain well and beat in half the butter.

5. Skin the fish fillets and cut in two if necessary. Use the rest of the butter to coat two heatproof plates and put the fillets on one and cover them with the other. Place the plates over a pan of boiling water and steam for 20 minutes or until cooked through.

6. For the sauce, melt the butter then stir in the flour to make a roux. Gradually stir in the milk. Bring to the boil. Reduce the heat and season. Cook for 1 minute, remove from the heat and stir in the cheese.

7. Cut out the puffed inside of the pastry boxes and use for lids. Divide the spinach between the boxes, lay the sole on top and add the sauce.

Singapore Fish

SERVES 6

The cuisine of Singapore was much influenced by that of China. In turn, the Chinese brought ingredients like curry powder into their own cuisine.

PREPARATION: 25 mins
COOKING: 10 mins

460g/1lb white fish fillets
1 egg white
1 tbsp cornflour
2 tsps white wine
Salt and pepper
Oil for frying
1 large onion, cut into 1.25cm/½-inch thick
  wedges
1 tbsp mild curry powder
1 small can pineapple pieces, drained and juice
  reserved
1 small can mandarin orange segments,
  drained and juice reserved
1 tbsp cornflour mixed with juice of 1 lime
2 tsps sugar (optional)
1 small can sliced water chestnuts, drained
Pinch salt and pepper

Step 1 Hold a filleting knife at a slight angle and slide the knife along the length of the fillet in a sawing motion.

1. Starting at the tail end of the fillets, skin them using a sharp knife. Hold the knife at an angle and, using a sawing motion, cut along the length of each fillet, pushing the fish flesh along as you go. Cut the fish into even-sized pieces, about 5cm/2 inches.

2. Mix together the egg white, cornflour, wine, salt and pepper. Place the fish in the mixture and leave to stand while heating the oil.

3. When the oil is hot, fry a few pieces of fish at a time until light golden brown and crisp. Remove the fish to kitchen paper to drain.

4. Remove all but 1 tbsp of the oil from the wok and add the onion. Stir-fry for 1-2 minutes and add the curry powder. Cook for a further 1-2 minutes. Add the juice from the pineapple and mandarin oranges and bring to the boil.

5. Combine the cornflour and lime juice and add a spoonful of the boiling fruit juice. Add the mixture to the wok and cook until thickened, about 2 minutes. Taste and add sugar if required. Add the fruit, water chestnuts, seasoning and fried fish to the wok and stir to coat. Heat through for 1 minute and serve immediately.

Snapper with Fennel and Orange Salad

This makes a lovely summer meal. Substitute another kind of fish if you can't get snapper.

PREPARATION: 30 mins
COOKING: 6-10 mins

Oil
4 even-sized red snapper, cleaned, heads and
   tails on
2 heads fennel
2 oranges
Juice of 1 lemon
3 tbsps olive oil
Pinch sugar, salt and black pepper

1. Brush the fish all over with oil and cut three slits into both sides of each. Sprinkle with a little of the lemon juice.

2. Core the fennel then slice thinly. Slice the

Step 2 Slice the fennel in half and remove the cores.

Step 3 Segment the oranges over a bowl to catch the juice.

green tops and chop the feathery fronds to use in the dressing.

3. Using a sharp knife, cut off all the peel and white pith from the oranges. Cut the flesh into segments slicing in between the membranes. Hold the fruit over a bowl to catch the juice.

4. Add the rest of the lemon juice to the orange juice in the bowl. Add the oil and seasonings. Mix well and add the fennel, green tops and orange segments, stirring carefully.

5. Cook the fish under a preheated medium hot grill 3-5 minutes per side, depending on thickness. The flesh will flake easily when it is cooked. Serve with the salad.

Seafood Torta

SERVES 6-8

A very stylish version of a fish flan, this makes a perfect lunch with some salad.

PREPARATION: 40 mins, plus chilling time
COOKING: 40 mins

Pastry
225g/8oz plain flour, sifted
Pinch salt
120g/4oz unsalted butter
60ml/4 tbsps cold milk

Filling
120g/4oz white fish fillets (plaice, sole or cod)
140ml/¼ pint water
140ml/¼ pint white wine
Large pinch dried flaked chillies
225g/8oz cooked prawns
120g/4oz dressed crab
30g/1oz butter
2 tbsps flour
1 clove garlic, crushed
2 egg yolks
140ml/¼ pint double cream
1 tbsp chopped fresh parsley

1. To prepare the pastry, sift the flour and salt into a bowl. Rub in the butter until the mixture resembles breadcrumbs. Pour in the milk and mix with a fork to a dough. Form a ball and knead for about 1 minute. Chill for about 1 hour.

2. To prepare the filling, cook the fish in the water and wine with the chilli flakes for about 10 minutes or until just firm. Remove from the liquid and flake into a bowl. Add the prawns and crab. Reserve cooking liquid.

3. Melt the butter in a saucepan and stir in the flour. Gradually strain on the cooking liquid, stirring constantly until smooth. Add garlic, place over high heat and bring to the boil and cook for 1 minute. Add to the fish and set aside to cool.

4. Roll out the pastry and use to line a loose bottomed flan tin. Prick lightly with a fork and chill for 30 minutes. Place greaseproof paper inside the case and fill with rice or baking beans. Bake for 15 minutes in an oven preheated to 190°C/375°F/Gas Mark 5.

5. Combine the egg yolks, cream and parsley and stir into the filling. When the pastry is ready, remove the paper and beans and pour in the filling.

6. Bake for a further 25 minutes. Allow to cool slightly and remove from the tin.

Skate Wings with Butter Sauce

SERVES 4

Skate wings are both economical and delicious, and make an interesting change from everyday fish dishes.

PREPARATION: 10-15 mins
COOKING: 20 mins

---

4 wings of skate
1 very small onion, sliced
2 parsley stalks
6 black peppercorns
280ml/½ pint vegetable or fish stock
60g/2oz unsalted butter
1 tbsp capers
2 tbsps white wine vinegar
1 tbsp fresh chopped parsley

---

1. Place the skate wings in one layer in a large, deep frying pan. Add the onion slices, parsley stalks and peppercorns, then pour over the stock.

Step 3 Carefully remove any skin or large bones from the cooked fish using a small sharp pointed knife.

Step 4 Add the vinegar to the hot butter and capers. This will cause the butter to foam.

2. Bring gently to the boil with the pan uncovered and allow to simmer for 10-15 minutes or until the fish is cooked and tender.

3. Carefully remove the skate wings from the pan and arrange on a serving platter. Remove any skin or large pieces of bone, taking great care not to break up the fish. Keep warm.

4. Place the butter into a small pan and cook over a high heat until it begins to brown. Add the capers and immediately remove the butter from the heat. Stir in the vinegar to foam the hot butter.

5. Pour the hot butter sauce over the skate wings and sprinkle with some chopped parsley. Serve immediately.

Stuffed Sole

SERVES 6

This German dish is elegant enough for a formal dinner party.

PREPARATION: 30 mins
COOKING: 20-30 mins

120g/4oz butter
2 tbsps flour
420ml/¾ pint fish or vegetable stock
90g/3oz button mushrooms, sliced
60ml/4 tbsps double cream
2 tbsps brandy
180g/6oz peeled, cooked prawns
120g/4oz canned, frozen or fresh crabmeat
30g/1oz fresh breadcrumbs
Salt and pepper
6-12 sole fillets, depending upon size, skinned

1. Melt half the butter in a saucepan. Stir in the flour and cook for about 2 minutes over gentle heat or until pale straw coloured. Stir in the stock and bring to the boil. Add the mushrooms and allow to cook until the sauce thickens.

2. Add the cream and re-boil the sauce.

Step 3 Spread stuffing on one side of each fillet and roll up. Secure with cocktail sticks.

Remove the sauce from the heat and stir in the brandy, prawns, crab, breadcrumbs and some seasoning.

3. Cut the fish fillets in half lengthwise and spread the filling on the side of the fish that was skinned. Roll the fish up and secure with cocktail sticks.

4. Arrange in a buttered baking dish, and dot the remaining butter over the top. Cook in an oven preheated to 180°C/350°F/Gas Mark 4, for 20-30 minutes, until the fish is just firm.

Baked Stuffed Mackerel

SERVES 4

In this recipe the combination of thyme and parsley in the stuffing beautifully complements the flavour of the mackerel. Herrings would also work well with the combination.

PREPARATION: 10 mins
COOKING: 25-30 mins

60g/2oz butter
1 small onion, finely chopped
1 tbsp oatmeal
120g/4oz breadcrumbs
1 heaped tsp freshly chopped thyme or ½ tsp dried
1 heaped tsp freshly chopped parsley or ½ tsp dried
Salt and pepper
2-3 tbsps hot water
4 mackerel, well cleaned and washed
1 lemon for garnish

---

1. Heat the butter in a frying pan, add the onion and sauté to soften. Add the oatmeal, breadcrumbs, herbs and seasoning. Mix well then bind together with the hot water.

2. Fill the cavities of the fish with the stuffing and wrap each one separately in well-buttered foil.

3. Place the parcels in a roasting tin or on a baking sheet and bake in an oven preheated to 190°C/375°F/Gas Mark 5, for 25-30 minutes or until cooked through and firm to the touch. Serve with lemon slices and thyme.

Swedish Herrings

SERVES 4

The Swedes adore the flavour of fresh dill and mild mustard. This combination is all that is required to bring out the full flavour of fresh herring.

PREPARATION: 10 mins
COOKING: 10-12 mins

15g/4 tbsps fresh chopped dill
90ml/3 fl oz mild Swedish mustard
2 tbsps lemon juice or white wine
4-8 fresh herrings, cleaned, but heads and tails left on
30g/1oz unsalted butter, melted
Freshly ground black pepper
Lemon wedges and whole sprigs of fresh dill, to garnish

---

1. Put the dill, mustard and lemon juice or white wine into a small bowl and mix together thoroughly.

2. Using a sharp knife, cut three shallow slits

Step 2 Using a very sharp knife, cut 3 shallow slits just through the skin on each side of the fish.

Step 3 Spread the mustard mixture over each fish, carefully pushing a little into each cut.

through the skin on both sides of each fish.

3. Spread half of the mustard mixture over one side of each fish, pushing some of the mixture into each cut.

4. Drizzle a little of the melted butter over the fish and cook under a preheated hot grill for 5-6 minutes.

5. Using a fish slice, carefully turn each fish over and spread with the remaining dill and mustard mixture.

6. Drizzle over the remaining butter and grill for a further 5-6 minutes, or until the fish is thoroughly cooked.

7. Sprinkle the fish with black pepper and serve garnished with dill sprigs and lemon wedges.

Swordfish with Garlic Sauce

SERVES 4

Swordfish steaks are delicious and are now easily available at most good fishmongers.

PREPARATION: 25 mins plus overnight
    marinating
COOKING: 10-15 mins

---

2 tbsps fresh green peppercorns
90ml/6 tbsps lemon juice
60ml/4 tbsps olive oil
Freshly ground sea salt
4 swordfish steaks
1 egg
1 clove garlic, roughly chopped
140ml/¼ pint oil
2 sprigs fresh oregano leaves, finely chopped
Salt and freshly ground black pepper

---

1. Crush the green peppercorns lightly using a pestle and mortar. Mix together the lemon juice, olive oil and salt.

2. Place the swordfish steaks in a shallow

Step 1 Lightly crush the green peppercorns using a pestle and mortar.

Step 3 Marinate the swordfish steaks overnight, after such time they should be opaque.

ovenproof dish and pour the lemon and oil mixture over each steak. Refrigerate overnight, turning occasionally until the fish becomes opaque.

3. Using a blender or food processor, mix together the egg and garlic.

4. With the machine still running, gradually pour the oil through the funnel in a thin steady stream onto the egg and garlic mixture. Continue to blend until the sauce is thick.

5. Preheat a grill to hot and arrange the swordfish on the grill pan, sprinkle over the oregano and season well. Cook for 10-15 minutes under a preheated hot grill, turning them frequently and basting with the lemon and pepper marinade.

6. When the steaks are cooked, place on a serving dish and spoon the garlic mayonnaise over to serve.

Fish Milanese

SERVES 4

These fish, cooked in the style of Milan, have a crispy crumb coating and the fresh tang of lemon juice.

PREPARATION: 10 mins plus 1 hr marinating
COOKING: 6 mins

---

4 large or 8 small sole or plaice fillets, skinned
2 tbsps dry vermouth
90ml/6 tbsps olive oil
1 bay leaf
Seasoned flour, for dredging
2 eggs, lightly beaten
Dry breadcrumbs
Oil for shallow frying
90g/3oz butter
1 clove garlic, crushed
2 tsps chopped parsley
1 tsp chopped fresh oregano
2 tbsps capers
Juice of 1 lemon
Salt and pepper
Lemon wedges and parsley, to garnish

---

1. Place the fish fillets in a large, shallow dish. Combine the vermouth, oil and bay leaf in a small saucepan and heat gently. Allow to cool completely and pour over the fish. Leave the fish to marinate for about 1 hour, turning them occasionally.

Step 3 Dip or brush the fillets with the beaten egg and press on the breadcrumb coating firmly.

2. Remove the fish from the marinade and dredge lightly with the seasoned flour.

3. Dip the fillets into the beaten eggs to coat, then into the breadcrumbs, pressing the crumbs on firmly.

4. Heat the oil in a large frying pan. Add the fillets and cook slowly for about 3 minutes on each side, until golden brown. Remove and drain on kitchen paper.

5. Pour the oil out of the frying pan and wipe it clean. Add the butter and the garlic and cook until both turn a light brown.

6. Add the herbs, capers, lemon juice and seasoning and pour immediately over the fish. Garnish with lemon wedges and sprigs of parsley.

Salmon Flan

SERVES 4-6

Canned salmon or tuna also make a good filling for this flan.

PREPARATION: 20-25 mins
COOKING: 40 mins

175g/6oz puff pastry
2 tsps cornflour
140ml/¼ pint milk
Salt and pepper
175g/6oz cooked fresh salmon
1 egg, lightly beaten
Dill, for garnish

1. Roll the pastry out into a square large enough to line a greased 20cm/8-inch flan dish. Trim off the excess pastry and crimp the edges.

2. Mix the cornflour with 1 tbsp of the milk, bring the rest to the boil, pour a little into the cornflour mix, stir well and add to the pan.

3. Return to the boil and cook for 1 minute, stirring constantly. Season well with salt and pepper and add 15g/½oz of butter. Remove the pan from the heat and add the egg, beating it in thoroughly.

4. Flake the salmon, removing any bones and skin, fold it into the sauce and spoon into the pastry case. Bake in an oven preheated to 190°C/375°F/Gas Mark 5, for 35-40 minutes, or until the filling is firm and the pastry golden. Serve garnished with dill sprigs.

Marinated Trout with Egg Sauce

SERVES 4

In this delicious recipe from Spain, the simply-prepared sauce allows the flavour of the fish to shine through.

PREPARATION: 10 mins, plus 30 mins marinating
COOKING: 20 mins

4 even-sized trout, cleaned but heads and tails left on
90ml/6 tbsps red wine
3 tbsps olive oil
3 tbsps water
1 clove garlic, crushed
2 sprigs fresh mint, 1 sprig fresh rosemary, 1 sprig fresh thyme, 1 small bay leaf, crumbled
6 black peppercorns
Pinch salt
3 egg yolks, lightly beaten
1 tbsp fresh chopped herbs
Lemon or lime slices, to garnish

1. Place the fish in a roasting tin and pour over the wine, oil, water, garlic and herbs. Sprinkle over the peppercorns and the salt and turn the fish several times to coat them thoroughly. Leave at room temperature for 30 minutes.

2. Place the roasting tin with the fish on top of the stove and bring the marinade just to the simmering point. Cover the tin and place in a preheated 180°C/350°F/Gas Mark 4 oven and cook for about 20 minutes or until firm.

Step 3 When the fish is cooked, transfer to a serving dish and peel off one side of the skin on each fish.

3. Transfer the fish to a dish and peel the skin off from one side. Cover and keep warm.

4. Strain the cooking liquid into a bowl set over a pan of hot water or into the top of a double boiler and discard the herbs and garlic. Mix about 3 tbsps of the liquid into the egg yolks and then return to the bowl or double boiler.

5. Heat slowly, whisking constantly until the sauce thickens. Do not allow the sauce to boil. Add the herbs and adjust the seasoning.

6. Coat the sauce over the skinned side of each trout and garnish the plate with lemon or lime wedges. Serve the rest of the sauce separately.

Mediterranean Shellfish Casserole

SERVES 4

Fresh shellfish cooked with red wine and tomatoes makes an impressive main course to serve for a special dinner party.

PREPARATION: 15-20 mins
COOKING: 30 mins

---

1 onion, finely chopped
3 tbsps olive oil
3 cloves garlic, crushed
680g/1½lbs tomatoes, skinned, seeded and
  chopped
2 tbsps tomato purée
570ml/1 pint dry red wine
Freshly ground black pepper
1.14 ltrs/2 pints mussels, in their shells
8 king prawns in their shells
120g/4oz peeled prawns
120g/4oz white crabmeat
8 small crab claws, shelled
2 tbsps vegetable oil
1 tbsp fresh chopped parsley
8 slices stale French bread

---

1. In a large saucepan, sauté the onion gently in the olive oil for 3 minutes, or until transparent but not browned.

2. Add 2 cloves of the garlic and the tomatoes. Sauté gently for a further 3 minutes, stirring to break up the tomatoes.

3. Stir in the tomato purée, red wine and black pepper. Bring the sauce to the boil; cover and simmer for 15 minutes.

4. Scrub the mussels to remove any small

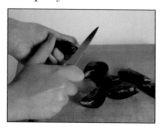

Step 4 Trim any small barnacles or pieces of seaweed away from the mussel shells using a small, sharp knife.

barnacles or bits of seaweed attached to the shells.

5. If any of the mussels are open, tap them gently with the handle of a knife. If they do not close up immediately, discard.

6. Drop the mussels into the tomato sauce. Cover and cook for 5 minutes.

7. Add the whole prawns, peeled prawns, crab and claws to the mussels and tomatoes. Re-cover and simmer for 5 minutes.

8. Heat the vegetable oil in a frying pan and stir in the remaining garlic and parsley.

9. Put the bread into the hot oil and fry until well browned.

10. Spoon the fish stew into a deep serving dish and arrange the garlic croûtes over the top. Stir briefly before serving.

Grilled Sardines with Romescu

SERVES 4

Romescu is a Spanish sauce that evolved from a fish stew recipe. It is simple to make and has a strong taste.

PREPARATION: 20 mins
COOKING: 10 mins

Romescu (Almond and Hot Pepper Sauce)
1 tomato, skinned, seeded and chopped
3 tbsps ground almonds
½ clove garlic, crushed
½ tsp cayenne pepper
Pinch salt
3 tbsps red wine vinegar
175ml/6 fl oz olive oil

900g/2lbs whole sardines, cleaned
Salt and pepper
Bay leaves
Olive oil
Lemon juice

1. To prepare the sauce, combine all the ingredients, except the vinegar and olive oil in

Step 1 Mix all the ingredients together into a smooth paste using a mortar and pestle.

Step 2 Once half the oil has been added, add the remainder in a thin, steady stream, whisking by hand.

a mortar and pestle and work until smooth.

2. Transfer to a bowl, whisk in red wine vinegar and add the oil gradually, a few drops at a time, mixing vigorously with a whisk or wooden spoon. Make sure each addition of oil is absorbed before adding more. Once about half the oil is added, the remainder may be poured in a thin, steady stream. Adjust the seasoning and set the sauce aside.

3. Wash the fish well, sprinkle the cavities with salt and pepper and place in a bay leaf. Brush the skin with olive oil and sprinkle with lemon juice. Cook under a preheated grill for about 2-3 minutes per side, depending on the thickness of the fish. Brush with lemon juice and olive oil while the fish is grilling. Serve with the sauce.

Index